REAL WORK

REAL WORK

poems

Janna Knittel

NODIN PRESS

Cover photo: Janna Knittel

Library of Congress Control Number: 2022946075

9 8 7 6 5 4 3 2 1

ISBN: 978-1-947237-50-6

Published by
Nodin Press
210 Edge Place,
Minneapolis, MN 55418
www.nodinpress.com

Printed in USA

For my sister

"This is what keeps you and me alive. This is the real work of the river."

– Alice Oswald, *Dart*

Contents

III

EPILOGUE

REAL WORK

PROLOGUE

ON RIVERS

St. Croix, Kickapoo
Namekagon:
You paddle history
weighing like water,
watched by eagles perched
in broken trees, led
by periscoping otters.

How smoothly you run
a river rests upon
your tools. Pack
knives for cutting lines.
Dry bags, life jackets
for shocking swims.
Know tools alone
can't save you
if you fail to use
them, use them wrong.

Resist your instinct
to focus on the downward
blade, pull yourself upriver.

In a kayak, you push
the upper hand
against the wind.

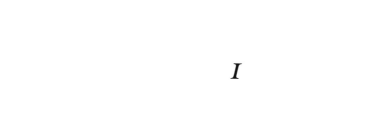

I

Do You Remember

Sleeping in the truck
on long drives home from camping,
how rumble and rock swayed you
into dreams, how adult voices
murmuring from front seats
were both blanket and pillow,
how light-dark-light fluttered
just outside consciousness
when you passed through towns,
how you woke to crunch
of gravel driveway not knowing
what time was and staggered
upstairs to bed? Your skin
holds memories of sun,
coldness of lake water. You hear
the rubber rowboat squeak,
rasp of sand on bare feet, chipmunks
inviting themselves to meals.
Each year you relearn
how mountain nights deliver
chill along with stars,
campfire smoke soaks clothes,
how you never would grow up
to be someone who did not remember.

MERCY

On Deer Creek, my father forced
a hook into salmon eggs,

pink and orange, threw
out a cast, then handed

me my child-sized rod.
We waited and reeled,

for years.
A tightening on my line:

I needed help to pull in
what had caught my hook.

When I saw that sunfish
struggle on a sunny rock

I begged him, *Let it go.*
My dad, who knew brutality,

whose parents changed their locks,
whose mother stabbed

him with a fork,
their legacy his will

to hit a child hard
enough to leave a mark.

Wordless, he pushed
the hook through

the fish's lip, clipped
the barb, slid

its grateful body
into the current.

MY FAVORITE AUNT

She taught me
to roll cigarettes
in her mobile home:
Lick your thumb
so it will stick
and let you lift a leaf
of rolling paper
from the packet.
Feed it to the rollers
of the hand-cranked
machine on
the kitchen table. Pinch
tobacco strands
from the pouch.
Then the hardest part:
to sprinkle it,
an even row
along the length of Zig Zag.
Don't make it fat
as her dog, Boozer,
in the middle, or let
the ends stay skinny
like his legs.
Turn the crank to wrap
the cylinder.
Release it. Lick
long edge of the paper,
press to seal.
I was sometimes
scared of her, gruff-voiced
from unfiltered
cigarettes,
tough as tobacco stains.
Her arms hugged me
near to death.

Rara Avis

He arrived in our first-grade classroom, two months late,
wearing gray-green trousers, matted cardigan.
The teacher told him to share my desk
while I thought: *Please. Don't.*

Days later, with cupcakes from Dari Mart,
we climbed through the skylight in his room,
surveyed our realm of roofs.
That night his dad read *Treasure Island*
while I dozed in a sleeping bag on the floor,
their tabby nibbling my fingers.

The whole family looked just roused
from camp, hair unruly as stacks
of hay in the sun. He and his sister played
violin. Both made me laugh
until I thought I'd split my skin.

My parents moved. My new school
might well have been in Iceland.
We diverged, grew up, he died,
before I expressed, among the gulls,
crows, jays of our small town,
he was an avocet.

My Parents' Luck

Her father was cold. His brutal.
Born into the Great Depression
they knew how to drill
new notches in their belts, callous
their palms. Yet they could ask
an ATM for 40 dollars
and get 60 bucks.

As students in Seattle,
they walked everywhere. One raw day,
my dad complained of cold hands.
There lay an expensive leather glove
on the sidewalk. *Too bad
it's not a pair!* They laughed, walked on.
Found its mate. They lived

through 13 recessions.
In '73, the worst, a federal
salary slipped from steak
once in a while to Hamburger
Helper for families of five.
They persisted. Each time
their life raft capsized they climbed

right back on. For a lark,
my mother visited a farm
for sale and fell enchanted.
For a lark, they bid,
lost to another buyer.
Days later, their phone rang:
The property is yours.

Two times, their luck staggered:
In '79, when ice ravaged

the orchard and their children's
college tuition. When their first
daughter died. I dared to ask
if she was all right. She said,
It would take more than that
to bring your father and I down.

Buying the Farm

My mother's whim while buying U-Pick berries
on a farm on Kiger Island
was to buy our own 14 acres of snags.

No city kids, my parents. Between her childhood
in Iowa, his summers
in hop fields, they surely knew the ropes,

but what a shaky vessel. Kristin cried.
I pretended, when
they said we'd leave Elmwood Drive for Route 3.

On wet winter days, the whole house hunched, crept
with shadows. We baked batches
of snickerdoodles in the yellow kitchen.

Frozen pipes. Leaky faucets. We found
our cat's kittens warming
by the water heater. Pastel fragments

of Easter eggs devoured by raccoons
and skunks. Easter colors
in my father's eyes as he posed for photos on the tractor.

In Deep

Visiting the farmhouse before moving day,
we found the downstairs bedroom flooded

by a bathroom faucet leak. An inch of water soaked
already sickly-green carpet.

Why do we have to move here?
My seven-year-old stomach sank

into the basement and mildewed.
Outside the ramshackle house,

a fruit tree grove out back
had served as dump for generations.

Fertile soil interred scraps
from several lives, now choked

by blackberry brambles, thick as my father's thumbs.
The smartest thing my parents did

was buy Kristin the dairy goat she wanted.
The yellow-eyed red Nubian chewed

paths through tangles, as treasures
emerged: cast-metal truck, Kewpie doll,

a hundred aggies and cat's eyes.
They let me tramp through this archeological dig.

Broken glass, cans rusted thin, shoe soles
no use to anyone, but I liberated

antique bottles, green and blue,
bits of painted porcelain, more abandoned toys.

After soaking in soapy water, some stood
on kitchen shelves, a mini museum.

Years later, what we still called *the thicket*
held trees plum-full of blossoms,

then plums. Slate path,
bird feeders, rhododendrons.

Bodies of farm cats, embraced
by graves marked with rounded stones.

HOMESTEADING

Imagine being sent to school
holding a wicker basket—
not a Snoopy lunchbox—
a ribbon on the handle, too.
The year my family moved
from town to farm, our mom
became Ma Ingalls, read all
the Little House books
to us as we burrowed
under quilts in our Arctic
attic bedroom, cats and hot
water bottles nestled at our feet.
She sewed calico dresses
and sunbonnets, paraded
us for family photos.
For the town's fall festival,
a neighbor made us costume
up to ride in the back
of his company truck: *Stu's
Manure*. Crowds of faces
laughed when he raised
the bed as if to dump us.
I don't remember if I told
my mom how tough the kids
at my new school were.
I do remember my basket
carried notes from her,
hard-boiled eggs with tiny
canisters of Morton Salt,
rolls of sweet-tart candies.

WESTERN FISH TOXICOLOGY STATION, CORVALLIS, OREGON

Let's see if my fish are dying,
Dad joked on weekends
when he invited me to his lab,
my strange playground.

Arranged in rows and columns,
filling a warehouse,
troughs of water cradled fry and parr.
From end to end of each I ran to see
clouds of fish reverse and flow away.
The air smelled of fish, fertilizer, river water.
Cuthroat, steelhead, rainbow trout,
Chinook, sockeye, coho salmon
mouthed words to songs
I couldn't hear
above the bubbling tank-din.

Outside, round fiberglass tanks
big as the downtown park fountain
held colossal fish, swimming circles,
iridescent carousels.

One summer, hotter than cigarette ash,
three kids whined and carped
until Dad tossed us in the truck,
drove to the lab, filled
an empty outdoor tank, hoisted
us over. Shocked by cold, we gaped,
then round and round, my sisters
and I kicked and flipped,
weightless, deep in green.

My Father's Hands

Visiting the dairy goat farm, I stepped out
the farmhouse door and fell down

the hole in the front porch
the owner forgot to mention.

I landed on a dirt pile,
made sure my eyes were open

because blackness bewildered me.
I remember flash of hurt

from tailbone up my spine,
how afraid I was of bats.

I sat on that hillock for less
than a minute but for thirty seconds

I believed they'd leave without me.
I was a penny down a well,

a scrap blown across a lake.
Until I tipped my head back

and saw rectangle of light,
my father's hands.

He pulled me out, asked,
Are you all right? I said *Yes,*

even though I didn't know,
my teeth still resonating.

I still don't know. No matter
how many days I lift myself up

two flights of stairs, return home
barely scathed, I still walk out

my door each morning, afraid
I'll drop and never stop.

One Day a Year I Liked Going to Church

In late summer, we retreat
to an outdoor sanctuary,
the woods behind First Congregational.

Two men build fires, spear
whole salmon, laid flat, roast them
over coals, coastal Native style.

Families offer bread and Jell-O,
cake and potato salad. Before
the meal, kids grow wings on their Keds,

scatter down dirt paths. Some leap
like stags through brush. We all ignore
warnings to keep our clothing dry, and hurtle

into the creek. We are lords
of crash and splash, skinned knees and palms,
seekers of periwinkles among pebbles.

Aside from the feast no one in church
talks about the Kalapuya,
the people who named Marys River and valley

Chepenefu, place of the elder-
berry. (I learned from a stone plaque.)
We clamber to picnic tables. Christ's fishes swim

with Pacific salmon as church kids
and I down cup after Dixie cup
of Hawaiian Punch, our first, my last, communion.

WILLAMETTE HIGHWAY

We swapped fields of summer crops
and rain for high desert,
Crescent Lake.

Mom and Dad walked the beach
as we three swam.
Pumice shoreline, ponderosa.

Sometimes we rowed
to the island
where we roamed prehistory.

One day ablaze,
on our way home
we jumped

into the river,
so cold we traded
skin for scales.

MICROCOSM

Baby toads spilled
from under a log.

With a stick,
six-year-old me

smashed as fast
as they hopped.

When I told my mom
what I'd done

she asked *Why?*
with a look

that turned me
to monster

toad, the wartiest ever.
Since then, I've asked

Why? Same tone,
same facial contortions.

How could I explain
awe and horror

too enmeshed
to unknot?

How could I explain death
meant nothing

yet? Sometimes home
and school teach you

to hunch your back
against sticks,

hit back, hide tenderness
beneath logs.

In the Orchard

Hazelnut trees are bushes,
extra branches, suckers, pruned
to grow a central trunk.

Was I glad for those impostors
the day thunder from the east
became semi-truck tires on rutted freeway

before my older sister saw a hundred hooves
beat ground and pounded
closer. Twenty seconds

to grasp the nearest hazel, pull up,
hold onto lichen-laced bark,
watch a black and white river

roil beneath. If one or all
had failed to scramble
high enough, or slipped,

our game would have ended.
After the flood, we cried and ran
to Mom, feared

returning cows more than how close
to shattering we'd come.
We'd survive

childhood, despite bikes and rocks,
swings and trees, cows,
my father's driving.

After broken bones
and stitches written later,
this scene still marks

the first time we felt
less like trees
than paper.

The Rabbits

One black, one red. Soft-shy mostly,
they sprang in circles when they saw me.
Dad built a hutch on legs to keep them
safe from hawks and owls. I fed them
after the school bus spit me out,
except one day I dropped myself
in front of the TV. After dinner,
when in twilight the holly bush
reared up, a bear, my mother asked
if I fed the rabbits. I told
the truth, begged her to walk with me.
She huffed. *There's nothing out there. I have*
dishes in the sink. She sent me
with a flashlight that fed shadows.
I toppled bowls and water bottles,
ran inside afterwards. The next night
she asked, *Did you feed the rabbits?*
The window a black shield behind her.
I said, *Yes.*

Real Work

Pick up hazelnuts. Drop them in a bucket.
     Shovel rabbit poop. Spread it on the garden.
          Pull vegetables. Wash and chop them.

On a farm, you learn real early
     never say, *I'm bored.*
          There's nothing to do.

The winter I was eight or nine
     I helped replant ten acres when
          a silver thaw broke every tree.

Of course I whined. Other kids rode bikes,
     tossing rolled-up newspapers,
          played with other people's kids.

That didn't look tough as chopping firewood,
     shelling peas, or raking
          half a ton of maple leaves.

No rest for the wicked, my folks would say.
     I still think I don't work
          now my hands are callous-free.

II

OLDER SISTER

You were the kind of girl
who wore a cape to school.
Blue plaid wool. One hand-me-down
I never got. Your favorite
color: yellow. Who picks that?

You never forgave my being born,
jumped on me in the crib, threatened
me with poison in-between
playing *Wynken, Blynken, and Nod*,
sailing in our cumulous boat.
You let me try to milk Peaches,

your pet goat. I watched you
purse your lips as you read grown-up
books or drew cadenzas from
your violin. Never still,
your fingers walked note after note,
even on invisible strings.

My friends' sisters talked
about sex, nail polish, teen pop singers.

My Boudica. My Suetonius.
When the boys with spears for voices
laughed at you I tried to close
my ears and shattered, too.

Uncanny

How I look like him: my nose bump,
cheekbones, jaw, all genetic copies.
With short hair, without makeup,
I could pass for a young Martin,
above the neck. If someone noticed,
he flung his arm around my shoulders,
said, *I can't deny this one.* My mother
did deny I looked anything
like her, would cry, *She's your daughter, Marty!*
as if boy-girl me were Caliban,
washed on shore. No wonder I grew up
certain I was a fairy changeling.
My father propagated chestnut saplings.
Maybe I was a bud graft, inserted
into cut cleft of bark on one
parent tree, the rootstock.

WARDROBE

Here comes the dyke!
Here comes the dyke!

Sophomore skater boys serenade
as you exit the stairway, crawl
a lengthening hall,
fumble at your locker.
Their sneers yank
your clipper-cut hair.
Three pairs of eyes remove
your mohair jacket—
        men's, circa 1965—
Bundeswehr trousers—
        loden wool—
argyle socks, brown
suede saddle shoes. Naked,
you navigate another day.
Those boys in Levi's jackets,
checkered Vans, don't know
how you pine for Andrew,
stoner math genius with long hair,
rumpled shirts. If they did,
they'd still lack a lexicon
for you. You never tolerated labels
on your clothes, how they bite
your skin. All you can do is lie
down at night, unbuttoned
and unbeaten.

This Round, Wooden Box on My Desk

My father made it,
carving a block
on a mini lathe.

This one wears a lid
turned to
screw on snugly,

the grain, chestnut
to blond, sanded
smooth.

The wood feels cool
to fingertips
and lips.

Lignum vitae:
wood of life.
Named for resilience

when whipped by rain,
licked by wind.
Iron wood:

It sinks
in water.
I am not that hard.

Still scarred by
rages risen
from nowhere.

He could laugh then swear,
throw my cat
down basement stairs.

His hand smacked
my five-year-old face
more than once.

He sat on the edge
of my bed
and apologized

yet erupted again
until the day
I was fifteen,

stood looking up
all six-foot-three,
dared him

to hit again.
I am not so tough
as *lignum vitae*.

I cowered
and cried.
I am not so beautiful

as *lignum vitae*,
my scars
blood-red and keloid.

I can't even lock
my heart
tightly

as a screw-top
lid, but I keep
this box.

About Bees

I

My father tended
six hives. Months after
each harvest we still
dipped honey from five-
gallon canisters,
poured liquid sugar
onto toast, licked our
knives and fingers. Rich
in stickiness, we
gave away jars
and jars of amber.

II

One summer I was in college,
bees busied themselves near my window.
One-by-one, a handful floated
through. Outside, I found bees hovering
near a hole scarcely bigger
than their fuzzy bodies. Workers
emerged in turns. My ear to wall
heard, or felt, the rumbulation
of fifty thousand bees. I pictured
joists and beams dripping with honey,
floors sagging, the whole house ruined
by delicious treasure.

III

Only twice have bees stung me.
Nine or ten, I watched the harvest,
slurping honey-laden comb.

I didn't see the bee fly up
my bell-bottomed jeans.
When it tickled my knee,
I scratched. It bit.
Lucky for me it was honey-sated,
stung only lazily.

IV

Raised among bees, I don't fear them,
don't scream and flap my hands.

These days I am afraid
of colony collapse,

how fewer stings mean
empty fields and grocery shelves.

I wish I could recall the fate
of the attic bees: smoked out,

honey confiscated?
May their progeny

still forage for clover,
blackberry, hazelnut pollen.

Still spin dust
into liquid gold.

GRAND PORTAGE

As far as work goes,
to give talks and tours,
play guitar and sing *"En Roulant!"*,
bake and sew in Métis dress,
is easy. Right?

Then a tourist asks the name of
the river they've been following
(pointing to Lake Superior's shore),
or if the stockade was built
to keep out Indians.

You withstand the headwind
of daily questions because,
seeing fireflies
for the first time,
you think them animals' eyes
in the woods.

You're really here
to hike and paddle;
track moose (*moozoog*),
bear (*makwag*),
wolves (*ma'iinganag*).
You are tracked,
seeing fresh scat
when doubling back
on the Portage.

On the ferry to Isle Royale,
a Catholic priest offers tobacco
to the Little Spirit Cedar tree
the People named
Manito Geezhigaynce.

By summer's end you can start a fire
with flint and steel
but can't stop hearing
the man who said,
Where are the injuns?
We came to see some injuns.

As, on the Great Hall roof,
an Anishinaabe coworker,
with buzz-cut hair,
Park Service uniform,
hammered shingles.

CURRANT JELLY

Her jars looked like cut glass
in the light, the jelly's red
a silk scarf held to sun.
Just one current bush grew
by the kitchen door. Ripened
berries draped each branch
like elven Christmas baubles.
She boiled a liquor of fruit
and sugar, hung the obscene
jelly bag to strain it,
then poured liquid garnet
into glass. When time
came to sell the farm,
she sent me the last jar,
heirloom jewel. I meant
to preserve it. Once opened,
the jelly slipped easily
past my lips, riding
rafts of buttered toast.
Along the wall of jams
and jellies in the store,
I find Tiptree & Crosse
and Blackwell's, from England.
Nothing close to home.

THE FOX

This morning I am burying a fox
found next to the trail
through Talahi Woods.
Whatever snared him,
no blood, no mark
tells the story.
Once electrified, each hair
from nose to tail now rests.
I blanket his body with leaves.
He is quickly gone,
his russet coat designed
for autumn camouflage.
Why can't I shatter
into leaves and dust,
while he springs forth,
coat and tail aflame,
to disappear
inside fall foliage?

PROFANE ELEGY

I spent my childhood
trying to fit
into your clothes.
I loved to receive
your hand-me-down
patched jeans, calico
dresses, remember
their warm scent.

The next third of my life I ran
from you, monument
of straight A's, lab reports
meticulous as a medieval scribe's,
your violin ignited
by Brandenburg Concertos.

You won everything,
burned all.

I hadn't seen you
for more than five years
when you died.
How did you become
too steeped in zolpidem
to know up from down?

Who's the smart one now?

I don't know when I lost you
the first time. What happened
between us playing
dolls and barely speaking?

That hasn't stopped me
from placing a palm-sized stone
beside your name,
asking you to
Take my place.

But nothing hefts
this slab of bluestone
from my chest.

MY SISTER'S CLOTHES

I collect what I can pack or ship
while her widower watches.

Among vintage and ornate pieces
I suspect mordant damage
but the dresses still wearing tags
hurt me most.

As I lay wool coats
across a chair, her cats climb
over, pawing them.

Folds of velvet, silk, and gabardine
suffer from memory.
All clothes do. That's why closets
so often house ghosts.

I have no room in my own closet.
I take a black wool coat,
three dresses, brocade
jacket, silk blouses.
To give her ghost a home.

Reading My Sister's Autopsy Report

It's like looking into the sun.
I close one eye.

The day's correct,
the 6th of August,
but someone typed
2004. I remember
the night in 2012—
a spider's web
I can't erase
from my face—
when my father left
the message: *Kay*
has died. I opened
another beer to keep
my hands from emptiness.

Codeine: Present.
Opiates: Presumptive Positive,
so why no history of suicide,
drug or pill abuse?

Who was Medic 27,
who pronounced her dead?
I want an audience.

The medical examiner describes her
long, wavy, red-brown hair:
a romance novel heroine's.

Her heart, he types,
weighed 260 grams.
No comments.
I guess that's normal.

Am I normal?
Someone, weigh
my heart.

GRIEF

In middle school wood shop,
my sister jigsaw-cut a slab
of mahogany into a pig.
That cutting board saw heavy use
in our farmhouse kitchen,
for chopping hazelnuts, zucchini, apples.

After her death, my parents ship it
—I hoard the memories I can—

but it fails to arrive.
The post office manager says
it's scanned. It reached the sorting station,
days ago. Probably stuck
on the belt, riding around,
around, around.

What do I do?

Wait. He shrugs.
All you can do is wait.

TALKING TO MY MOTHER ON THE PHONE,
TWO AND A HALF YEARS AFTER

Twig by twig and stone by stone
she's built a dam to impound the flow
of any mention of my sister's death.
One week, one month, one year, two years
into the loss, she packs her ears
with mud if I ask questions, mortars
her mouth against answers. We converse
around the confluence but never venture
near those swifter waters. I am inured
to logjams our conversations strike,
how she blocks me, with, *It's late*,
or *Nice to talk to you.* Tonight, before
we said goodbye, she opened a spillway,
saying, *Your dad and I are thinking of you.*
Take care of yourself. We're running
out of daughters.

VICODIN

Watching blue snowflakes fall
I wonder where I keep
the fishing knife
found piercing a log
along the Breitenbush River
two summers ago.
Windowpanes breathe consumptively.
If I get up to add
spinach to the list will I risk
scrolling messages for hours?
Bananas browning
on the kitchen counter
feel acutely lonely.
A red-haired poet read
my love poem, proclaimed
it about colonialism.
I can't reach the reins
of words once I set
them into tracks, can't steer
them through drifts or undergrowth.
Blue snow falls, heavier. Bluer.
The knife fits in my hand,
dislodges.

My Father at 80

It makes him look like he's been beaten
with a pipe, the Coumadin:
blooms of purple garland
each arm, the backs of his hands,
so he no longer looks invincible,
the Teutonic-Celtic hero
in letterman sweater, army uniform,
denim jacket brushmarked
with paint and tree seal.
I call him Rasputin behind his back
because he keeps outsmarting death
until I think he'll outlive me,
but lately he stoops, has lost
interest in working at the lathe,
mostly watches TV with his terrier
on his lap. Someday I have to kill
this illusion of immortality.
To me, he is still casting his line
into the Metolius and Siuslaw rivers,
tending beehives, pruning trees,
carving myrtlewood burls into bowls,
swimming faster than anyone.

GRIMOIRE

The spell for protection:
    hold a wren's egg
    under your tongue.

The spell for direction:
    cast salt
    to the four winds.

The spell for youth:
    walk backwards
    through a mirror.

The spell for wealth:
    hold a flame
    over all your clothing.

The spell for friendship:
    stand outside and whistle
    like a white-throated sparrow.

The spell for love:
    peel pine cones until
    your fingertips bleed.

The spell for courage:
    throw your knife
    into whitewater.

The spell for healing:
    lie down in a snowfall
    until drifts cover your eyes.

III

You Might Know ~~America~~

If you ever drove across midwestern plains
        on a road between two fields
        of sunflowers, maned faces
        roaring east, west, east,

hoping to spy bison, meeting only graves,
        at Custer National Battlefield.

If you rode the Empire Builder
        on rails between empire's boundaries:
        barbed wire fences festooned
        with plastic bags breathing
        in, breathing out,

and imagined a young man
        hanging from barbed wire.

If you mistook a church
        for a shopping center
        alit to guide you
        through darkness.

If you sweated through your clothes
        hiking the north woods
        in August, so Lake Superior's
        frigid waters looked like
        a silver medal.

If a lone coyote, camouflaged
        by pumice sand
        and sagebrush,
        saw you first, then
        loped across the desert.

If you climbed Mt. Jefferson
          to the song of
       jet engines.

THIN PLACES

Heaven and earth overlap.
You stand on an invisible bridge

between two worlds
loosely stitched.

You know it in a breath
when ordinary stones

in Scotland sweep
more magic through you

than Stonehenge. Or years drag
before you know

you touched the hem
of heaven.

After his triple bypass
I asked my father to visit

the wild bird refuge
where we walked between

moss-dressed trees,
where I held my breath,

where I photographed
him kneeling

beneath a curved-out
branch, after which

he lived 26 years
longer.

LAKE CELILO

Beneath the waters of Lake Celilo lies what
were once some of the most productive salmon
fishing sites in all of North America. ("The
Dalles Dam," Oregon History Project)

July sun burns hard, evidence
cherry trees never grew here
before the dam.

I have eaten those cherries, drenched
in syrup, piled in pies, gobbled
out of hand.

For centuries, the river billowed
over stacks of rocks, white
clouds, sound

of a thousand canoe paddles.
Now, east of The Dalles,
the Columbia folds

up behind the dam, water
flatter than a sheet
of aluminum

pressed out by the Alcoa plant.
Winds blow through
the gorge, pushing

sailboarders across its surface.
The lake is fake, generated
by the dam

which is why I stop to see it.
A fishing platform,
splintered wood,

stands alone. Three crows
drift down,
conspire.

Upriver at the in lieu fishing sites
I saw three crows, too,
maybe ravens.

Big black birds in groups
of threes must mean
something

in someone's tradition. I have no tradition,
except to fly west yearly to remember
where I'm from.

FIRST ANNIVERSARY

How should we mark
the 365 days
of this new phase?

No rituals feel
fitting to our
peculiar love.

I will light a candle,
bake kolaches,
while you look

over my shoulder.
I can walk
in the woods,

wear the belt
you gave me,
your knife,

talk to your ashes.
Tell me how to mark
this long year

since you left
on what you called,
the next adventure.

CANIS SOLO

I fly over tundra, my fur
sun-shot, gleaming obsidian.

The last wolf killed in Scotland
was black.

I feel like
the last wolf in Scotland.

I've been misnamed.
Some say my DNA

is a common cur's
but I am rare, so rare

hunters cannot find me
with their sights and rifles

as long as it is night.
I didn't always roam alone.

I once owned the tundra
with a mate

until I drove my fellow wolf
to seek new territory.

One day I will lay down
my pelt

in reconciliation.

Lost in the Library

Advice my mom bestowed includes,
You really should wear lipstick,
her opinions a card catalogue
surrounded by online databases,
yet I miss asking her:

Should I quit the job
that makes me grind my teeth?
Would she like the book I'm reading?

Lately, she can't follow me
down corridors not perfectly straight.
Lately, I don't ask for anything.

I seldom call, because she answers,
waits for me to speak, shouts,
Hello, hello, over me,
leaps from yesterday to years ago.

Like Arcimboldo's painting
she was built of books.
She had a spine.

Now, when she opens a volume,
pages spill from her grasp.
Common words hide
behind a brocade curtain.
She skips chapters in her story,
or turns back to the first, rereads.

When she asks me,
Have you talked to J?
I know for sure
she's leaving.

She erases the mistakes
she can. My dad helps
her. Fear of losing
all those books
forces her to pretend
she is still the reference librarian
everyone came to with questions.

Inheritance

As if it were wet clay,
he'd turn a block of myrtle,
mesquite, or madrone
on lathes, carve curves
from corners.

My favorite piece, a vase:
rivulet of light twined
through a knot,
flaw transformed.

Now, on the floor of his room:
all six drawers from the dresser
he crafted of cherry wood.

He says the drawers don't fit.
They stick. He's given up
the battle.

This ponderosa of a man
now bends,
a snow-bowed branch,
can't lift a slab of wood,
whether spruce or sequoia,
however beautifully grained.

Neither of us know
three tumors
grow in his brain
like amboyna burls.

I carry each drawer outside.
In the sun, I fight
rough edges,

swollen joints
with a coarse-grit
sanding sponge,
wear down
my arms to saplings.

Because he is my father,
love is carved in runes.
Because I am half him,
I know how to use
my hands: Attack,
defend, create.

Hammer, level, sand.

My Father's Brain

We see with our brains,
not our eyes, Dr. Bach-y-Rita says,

and the tumors binding
my father's occipital lobe

killed his sight faster
than the glaucoma.

As a microbiologist,
his job was to see

worlds within worlds.
The last time I saw him

try to read, he held *Time*
magazine upside-down.

Glioblastoma multiforme looks
like a crab, clawing

healthy brain. On an MRI
it's a radar image of a hurricane.

HOSPICE

I'd rather tame a bison bull
than ask,

> *Is there anything
> you want to say
> before I leave?*

But I do. He stares ahead,
eyes marbled.

> *Not particularly.*

I want to peel off my skin,
turn to smoke, ascend,
but I stay, massage his rusty hands
until I must chase a plane.

Over the highway, rags and ashes
reel, unfold,
into a current of crows.

A sign on the bridge
over the Clackamas
chastises:

*Undertow. Rocks.
Cold Shock.
Swim at Your Own Risk.*

MY FATHER'S ASHES

A handful flows downstream
toward the Columbia.
A handful drifts, like smoke,
from Crescent Lake's surface
to the floor. All of him rises
sky-far from his first appearance
in Wyoming, from running
laundry and picking hops in Oregon,
from a Washington, DC lectern.

I want a thimble-full to hold,
a keepsake in my pocket,
but remember this man lived
in five different states,
couldn't sleep the last night
we camped in Yellowstone,
so drove through Idaho until
my mom, my sisters, and I woke
at home where he remained
restless as a migrating salmon.

With my sole surviving sister
and her daughters, I watch him fall
through glacial water.
My youngest niece says,
Maybe he'll be eaten
by a fish who'll be eaten
by a bigger fish. I can't imagine
any honor he'd love more
unless we could have flown
him to the moon.

THE WORK (DREAMING OF MY FATHER)

From room to room
we inspect the farmhouse
as storms drape faulty roof.

A steady trickle
rains down one corner
in the first. Next,

insistent dripping.
The third room: submerged
in crisis. We wade through to

our knees. What do
we do while waiting
for experts and equipment?

Bail, he says.
Start bailing. With the tools

at hand, together
we bend, scoop,
pour kitchen bowls

of raindrops out
the window, as thousands
more bowls-full flow

inside. *Do the work*,
say his motions, even
when you fight a flood,

when your bowl
overflows.
Your work is your wage.

Skiing at Dusk

This loop through pine woods
winding round small lakes
takes two hours.

I have one hour of daylight
to see a circlet of blood,
sunset on snow,

rabbit or squirrel transformed
by beak and talons. Maybe
a least weasel—

phantom, white on white—peering
from behind a fallen branch.
Sunlight shafts

straight through trees, parallel to earth.
Snow phases from white to pink,
blue to violet: death

of light. I used to fear this time. Even now,
the wind reaches between me
and my clothes.

I want to ski faster. I could fall on my knees
at the feet of the sun
and sob

but I scroll down
the longest hill
with ease.

Where Rivers Meet

On a raw day striped
by sleet I walk the trail
around Pike Island, the land
the Dakota named Wita
Tanka. Wrapped in fleece
and fog I scan the woods
through lens of dusk.
All quiet. Rare not to see
the herd of deer that snort
at me most times I visit.
Then the reason emerges
from trees and drifts
across my field of vision:
two coyotes, wearing
smoke-ash robes, quiet
as slippered ghosts,
trot their rounds, hoping
for a meal, a bad day
for a rabbit. Their pelts
so dense no burrs can weasel
down to skin, paws larger
than my heart. That heart
pulses as they stride over
it then slip between
curtains of darkening woods.
Despite the island's smallness
I won't see them again,
can't trace their trail through grasses
or across the river.
I imagine each blade and drop
their coats brush tipped
with quicksilver.

The Diminutive Effect

Stand on a summit or with toes in the ocean.
Go where night sky wheels uncaring
above you. Where a tree reveals
your true size. Paddle to the middle
of the largest lake you know.
Feel how far you must swim
in any direction to save your own life.
On the trail, seek boulders taller
than your reach, wonder how far
glaciers carried them. Dare
to feel how small you stand. If
you think you can touch the sky,
keep climbing. Climb until you feel
farther than ever from heaven.

My Mother's Brain

The area of the brain
named by Broca births
language. The one

for Wernicke churns
it to meaning.
Somewhere between

these realms
a bridge collapsed.
Her dictionary shrank

from a librarian's
to nervous chuckles,
the word *coffee*.

Other threats stormed
her brain before
Dr. Alzheimer crept in.

Major depression,
electroshock. Who
knows when

her troubles began.
I sit with her,
read out loud.

She stares at me
or fumbles
with my jacket's zipper.

She will lose all knowledge
of how to eat,
to breathe.

I walk in the dark
with her, wonder if she knows
it's me.

KINGFISHER

Rattle-cries in flight. Hovers
over sleep-walking water
where river swirls
in dark depressions.
Seeks a perch. Alights. Resists.
Then spies
sticklebacks, stonerollers.
Deep into the kettle, dives,
through cold then colder layers.
Grasps wriggling slickness
in her dagger beak. Rises, rises,
jewel clasped between
two blades. On stone
she strikes the prize to shatter
bones before swallowing
her captive whole.
Cleans and hones her weapon
against branches.
In sunlight shakes
her feathers dry.

ALKALI LAKE

In the rain shadow, desert grows.
Lake is metaphor only.
Spring hopsage and rabbitbrush choke
on dirt-dust. Wild buckwheat

shrinks from sun. Kick rocks. Dig cracks
into the clay. You'll find
no water many miles down.
If you stay, your skin

will split. You could trek over mountains
and drown. Choose your path:
either deprivation or excess.
How many winters since

Hart Peak's shoulders wore a cape
of white? No god's at fault.
Your water bottle rolls away, empty.
The snow on the ground is salt.

ON THE TRAIL

You could cry into your rucksack now
you've eaten all the chocolate, lost
the trail. You are not lost: You are inside
Deschutes National Forest. The parking lot
is lost. The sky is hot, hotter than ever
you remember. Maiden Lake wore
a skirt of dried mud laced with algae. You cry
because you've lost the home you always knew,
thought you would reclaim. Fire chewed through
last summer and the summer before. The sun
punishes; you still follow its fist to measure
time, tell east from west. On a fallen log
within a mountain hemlock's shadow, rest
your back. Unpack. Repack: Water, map,
trail mix, your sister's love, four west coast friends
despite 20 years away, three friends
in the heartland. You're not on your knees.
You're strong enough to carry everything you need.

EPILOGUE

Doing the Work

Shove a black block of granite uphill.

*

Pull buckthorn. Knapweed. Garlic mustard.

*

Climb Eagle Mountain. Barefoot.

*

Count pine needles, ticks, microbes.

*

Decode the sharp-shinned hawk's flight patterns.

*

Fish for Chinook in Lake Superior.

*

Grasp the wind. Now with just one hand.

*

Eat clouds. Swallow thunder.

*

Tell a story everyone denies.

*

This water only looks shallow. Dive.

"You Might Know ~~America~~" is a protesting response to the February 16, 2016 tweet by Republican candidate for President Jeb Bush of a photo of his handgun with the single-word caption: "America."

"Lake Celilo" was written as part of a series of poems about the inundation of Celilo Falls, a group of several cascades and waterfalls on the Columbia River located approximately 13 miles east of what is now the town of The Dalles. Celilo was, for generations, a major fishery for Native peoples on both sides of the river. William Clark described it in a journal entry on October 24, 1805 but the site was a place of sustenance, trade, and community long before the Corps of Discovery arrived. Celilo was considered the oldest continuously inhabited community on the North American continent until 1957. In that year, Celilo Falls and surrounding villages were submerged by the construction of The Dalles Dam to provide hydroelectric power to the region and enable barge traffic on the Columbia River. In lieu fishing sites are fishing sites reserved for Native peoples since traditional sites were inundated.

"Lost in the Library" refers to *The Librarian* (oil on canvas, circa 1566) by Italian painter Giuseppe Arcimboldo (1526 or 1527-1593).

"My Father's Brain" quotes American neuroscientist Paul Bach-y-Rita (1934-2006), from his book *The Brain That Changes Itself.*

Acknowledgements

The following poems have been previously published—some in different form—in the following:

"Do You Remember." Parks and Points Poetry 2022.
"Hospice": *Breakwater Review.*
"On the Trail": *Lyricality.*
"Wardrobe" and "In Deep": *Constellations.*
"Vicodin": *Between These Shores Literary and Arts Annual.*
"First Anniversary," "Thin Places," and "Willamette Highway." *The Wild Word.*
"Where Rivers Meet": *Blueline.*
"About Bees": *Tiny Seed.*
"The Fox." *Up North Lit.*
"Profane Elegy"; "Talking to My Mother on the Phone, Two and a Half Years After"; and "Grief." *North Dakota Quarterly.*
"Lost in the Library": *After the Equinox.* Minneapolis, MN. Cracked Walnut, 2018.
"Grand Portage." *Waters Deep: A Great Lakes Anthology.* Ed. Crystal S. Gibbons and Michelle Menting. Two Harbors, MN: Split Rock Review, 2018.
"Driftless." *Split Rock Review.*
"Grimoire": *Whale Road Review.*
"On Rivers." *Thresholds.* Cracked Walnut: Minneapolis, MN, 2017.
"Western Fish Toxicology Station, Corvallis, Oregon" and "My Father at 80": *NEAT Magazine.*

The following poems were published in the chapbook *Fish & Wild Life* (Georgetown, KY: Finishing Line Press, 2018): "Mercy"; "Western Fish Toxicology Station, Corvallis, Oregon"; "*Canis Solo*"; "Skiing at Dusk"; and "Kingfisher."

This book has increasingly lived up to its title. It began as my MFA thesis for the University of Oregon, where Peter Campion, Patricia Kirkpatrick, and Kim Todd provided me with skillful creative guidance and hope that the project could become a book.

Two travel grants from the University of Minnesota College of Liberal Arts provided time for research and writing. Three grants from the Minnesota State Arts Board supported my work with much-needed funding for creative work and outreach to other poets and new audiences.

Elizabeth Woody gave guidance about researching Celilo Falls and the Oregon Historical Society provided access to historic documents about Celilo Village.

Patricia Kirkpatrick and Rachel Moritz each reviewed later versions of the manuscript, advising on everything from line edits to recommending the order of poems. If this manuscript bears little resemblance to what they read it is not because I did not follow their advice but because the poems and the shape of the book continued to change in ensuing years.

Jim Cihlar offered advice about the overall structure for the book, which was immensely helpful.

Peter Campion read the penultimate version of the manuscript and gave me much-needed confidence.

A group of poets that started meeting online during the beginning of the COVID-19 pandemic and has lasted until now—organized by Wendy Brown-Baez and including Debbi Brody, Christine Mounts, Diane Pecoraro, and Sarah Degner Riveros—kept me writing and inspired while I continued to hone the manuscript. A few poems begun or revised during those workshops appear in this volume.

I am grateful to Nodin Press for bringing this book to life. Norton Stillman believed in it and John Toren gave me time to revise the manuscript and allowed input on the cover design.

Friends sustained me more than they know. Even if I wasn't talking about my writing or sharing my writing with them, they helped me persist. Bonnie, Laura, Lesly, and Kay in Oregon; Ray and Stephen in Kansas; and Christa, Kit, and Melinda in Minnesota: Thank you.

For Laura M. Knittel most of all.

About the Author

Janna Knittel is from the Pacific Northwest and now lives in Minnesota. Janna's previous publications include the chapbook *Fish & Wild Life* (Finishing Line Press, 2018) and poems in *Between These Shores Literary and Arts Annual*, *Blueline*, *Breakwater Review*, *Constellations*, *Cottonwood*, *North Dakota Quarterly*, *Up North Lit*, *Whale Road Review*, and *The Wild Word*, among other journals, as well as the anthology *Waters Deep: A Great Lakes Anthology* (Split Rock Review, 2018). Janna has taught literature and writing classes at colleges and universities in Oregon, Kansas, and Minnesota, and has also published scholarly essays on literature.